Natsuki Hokami

While I was drawing, I remembered something: I really like those jelly drinks that you have to shake. There was a vending machine at the high school I went that sold a mango gelatin in the summer, and I bought a ton of them. I suppose those gelatins are probably gone by now.

Natsuki Hokami's first serialized manga, *Hell Warden Higuma*, was published in *Weekly Shonen Jump* in 2018.

Demon Slayer: Kimetsu Academy

VOLUME 2
SHONEN JUMP EDITION

STORY AND ART BY
NATSUKI HOKAMI

Translation / John Werry
Touch-Up Art & Lettering / E.K. Weaver
Design / Yukiko Whitley
Editor / Andrew Kuhre Bartosh

Printed in the U.S.A.

Published by VIZ Media, LLC
P.O. Box 77010
San Francisco, CA 94107

10 9 8 7 6 5 4 3 2 1
First printing, April 2024

The Kimetsu Academy Night Tour

Story and Art by

Natsuki Hokami

Based on Koyoharu Gotouge's *Demon Slayer: Kimetsu no Yaiba*

DEMON SLAYER KIMETSU ACADEMY CHARACTERS

NEZUKO KAMADO

TARO CLASS JUNIOR HIGH, SECOND-YEAR

Tanjiro's younger sister. Always groggy in the morning.

TANJIRO KAMADO

BAMBOO SHOOT CLASS HIGH SCHOOL, FIRST-YEAR

A serious and polite boy. Wears earrings even though it's against the rules.

ZENITSU AGATSUMA

A very moody guy. Part of the disciplinary committee despite Tomioka Sensei's suspicions that his hair is dyed.

BAMBOO SHOOT CLASS HIGH SCHOOL, FIRST-YEAR

INOSUKE HASHIBIRA

A hungry boy who loves tempura. Doesn't bother with books, just his lunch.

PEPPER CLASS SECOND-YEAR
MURATA

MUGWORT CLASS THIRD-YEAR
SHINOBU KOCHO

VIOLET CLASS SECOND-YEAR
KANAO TSUYURI

HIGH SCHOOL

JUNIOR HIGH

TARO CLASS SECOND-YEAR
MAKOMO

TARO CLASS SECOND-YEAR
MUICHIRO TOKITO

TEACHERS

MATH TEACHER
SANEMI SHINAZUGAWA

CIVICS TEACHER
BAMBOO SHOOT HOMEROOM TEACHER
GYOMEI HIMEJIMA

P.E. TEACHER
SPARTAN LIFE GUIDANCE
GIYU TOMIOKA

BIOLOGY TEACHER
KANAE KOCHO

HISTORY TEACHER
KYOJURO RENGOKU

ART TEACHER
TENGEN UZUI

THE STORY SO FAR

Tanjiro and his friends attend Kimetsu Academy, a private elementary, junior high, and high school. The teachers and students are a bunch of weirdos who turn classes into chaos!

GRADUATE

PIZZA DELIVERY GIRL
MITSURI KANROJI

CHEMISTRY TEACHER
OBANAI IGURO

CONTENTS

2 The Kimetsu Academy Night Tour

Chapter 6 Catnip for Kitties, Kitties for Himejima.....7

Chapter 7 The Secret of Hot Spring Eggs.....39

Chapter 8 The Squeal Equation.....71

Chapter 9 The Kimetsu Academy Night Tour.....103

Chapter 10 Love and Snakes.....135

Bonus Chapter Kumotori Station, 7:30 A.M......173

CHAPTER 6: CATNIP FOR KITTIES, KITTIES FOR HIMEJIMA

KIMETSU ACADEMY'S HIGH SCHOOL
GYOMEI HIMEJIMA
BAMBOO SHOOT CLASS HOMEROOM TEACHER
HOBBY: PLAYING THE SHAKUHACHI FLUTE
WHERE'RE YA GOIN', HIMEJIMA SENSEI?
TO GET A DRINK FROM THE CONVEN-IENCE STORE.
HUH? WHY NOT USE THE SCHOOL KIOSK?
Kyah! Uzui Sensei!
?
GYOMEI HAS A SECRET.

MEOW
AH!
GLANCE
GLANCE

I FOUND THIS CAT THE OTHER DAY.
IT'S BEEN WANDERING AROUND THE CAMPUS.
I THINK IT'S LOST.
It has a collar.
KRNCH KRNCH

AND IT IS SO...

...CUTE!

I LOVE EVERYTHING ABOUT CATS...
...FROM THE WAY THEY LOOK TO HOW THEY BEHAVE.
JUST PETTING ONE IS ENOUGH TO GIVE ME ENERGY BACK.

SIGH
I KNOW I SHOULDN'T BE CARING FOR IT IN SECRET...

...OR FEEDING IT ON SCHOOL GROUNDS, BUT...
PURR
PURR

THIS IS JUST UNTIL YOUR OWNER FINDS YOU!
PSS PSS
BESIDES, IT'S NOT LIKE ANY STUDENTS WILL FIND ME OUT HERE!

OH, HIMEJIMA SENSEI!!!!

HEYA, HIMEJIMA SENSEI!!

QUIETER, PLEASE.

WHATCHA DOIN' OUT HERE?!

NOT SO LOUD.

WOW! WHAT A CUTE KITTY!!

IS IT LOST?
ITS OWNER MUST BE WORRIED.
YEAH...
TANJIRO KAMADO
BAMBOO SHOOT CLASS
FIRST-YEAR
YOU SHOULDN'T KEEP SOMETHING LIKE THIS TO YOURSELF!
ZENITSU AGATSUMA
BAMBOO SHOOT CLASS
FIRST-YEAR
YEAH! THE WHOLE CLASS COULD HELP!
INOSUKE HASHIBIRA
BAMBOO SHOOT CLASS
FIRST-YEAR
WELL, SOME STUDENTS MIGHT BE ALLERGIC.
BESIDES ...

AFTER SCHOOL...

BAMBOO SHOOT CLASS
FIRST-YEAR

WELCOME TO THE 356TH SECRET MEETING...
...OF THE "FIND ROCKY'S OWNER" SOCIETY!!
ISN'T THIS THE FIRST MEETING?
Hey!
YOU HAVE TO RAISE YOUR HAND BEFORE SPEAKING!!
ME!!
FWIP
LIKE THAT! YES, INOSUKE?
I NEED MORE SNACKS!!
SWAP
SMALL DRIED SARDINES
THOSE WERE FOR ROCKY!
UM...
YES, HIMEJIMA SENSEI?

I MADE SOME MISSING POSTERS.

FOUND CAT

DESCRIPTION: CALICO MALE HAS A COLLAR

YEAH, THIS ISN'T GOING TO WORK.

IT'S ALL WORDS!

SCOFF SCOFF

OH, REALLY?

IT JUST NEEDS A PICTURE OF ROCKY!

MAYBE A DRAWING?

I CAN DO IT!*

HECK NO!

HOW ABOUT THIS PICTURE, THEN?

*CHECK VOLUME 1 TO SEE TANJIRO'S ARTISTIC "SKILLS."

OKAY, I'LL ADD THIS TO THE POSTER.
THEN WE CAN HANG THEM UP ALL AROUND SCHOOL!
WE'LL NEED TO GET PERMISSION FIRST.
CHAT
CHAT
!
YOU ALL SHOULD BE ON YOUR WAY HOME!!!
NO LOITERING WITHOUT A PROPER EXCUSE!!!
KYOJURO RENGOKU
HISTORY TEACHER
STARTLED
REN-GOKU...
OH!
HIMEJIMA SENSEI!!

YOU'RE WITH THEM?
SORRY 'BOUT THAT!
UM...
...WE WERE JUST FINISHING UP.
WHAT WERE YOU ALL TALKING ABOUT?
A CA—
PLUG
NOTHING!!!
WE'RE ALL READY TO GO!
DELISH BA
GRIN GRIN GRIN
SEE YOU LATER!!
??
OKAY! SEE YA!!

KEEPING SECRETS WITH STUDENTS ...
...IS IN-APPROPRIATE FOR A TEACHER.
Careful on the way home!
HEH HEH
BUT IT IS KINDA FUN.
THIS'LL BE A MEMORY TO TREASURE ONCE THEY GRADUATE.
PLIP PLIP
THE NEXT DAY...
TAK
FOUND
• CALICO
• MALE
• HAS A COLLAR
IF THIS IS YOUR CAT PLEASE CALL (XXX)XXX-X
THERE.
THAT SHOULD DO IT.
I...

...DON'T MIND HELPING OUT...
...BUT THAT CAT SEEMS WEIRDLY TAME.
DOESN'T BITE
DOESN'T SCRATCH
COMES WHEN CALLED
IS IT REALLY LOST?
PAT
PAT
AGA-TSUMA.
EEGYAAAAH!!!
T-T-TOMIOKA SENSEI?!
I GOT PERMISSION TO PUT THAT UP!!
AND MY HAIR'S NATURALLY BLOND!!
NEVER MIND THAT.

I SAW KAMADO AND HASHI-BIRA...
...PUTTING UP THE SAME NOTICE.
GIYU TOMIOKA
P.E. TEACHER

THE THREE OF YOU AREN'T SECRETLY KEEPING THIS CAT ON SCHOOL GROUNDS, ARE YOU?
BULLS-EYE

W-WHAT? NO! OF COURSE NOT!
I'D NEVER DO SOMETHING LIKE THAT! BUT ONE OF THOSE TWO MIGHT!
OH? THEN I'LL ASK THEM.
SKF
PHEW
I TOTALLY SOLD THEM OUT...
...BUT I'M SURE THEY'LL BE FINE.
PROB-ABLY.

ZEEEE-NITSUUU!!

AH HA HA HA HA

IT'S WAS RAINING, SO I BROUGHT THE CAT IN!

WHERE SHOULD WE KEEP IT?

TMP TMP TMP TMP
YOUR TIMING SUCKS!
MY BAD!!!

WHOA!
BOOOOSH
!
TAP
PAR-DON.
FMP
WSH
TMP TMP TMP
SORRY, TAMAYO SENSEI!
THAT CAT...
TAMAYO
SCHOOL NURSE
FWIP
FOUND CAT
OH DEAR...

I'LL DISTRACT TOMIOKA SENSEI!
YOU GO FIND HIMEJIMA SENSEI!
OKAY, GOT IT!!
VOOSH
VOOSH
HIMEJIMA SENSEI?
SOICHIRO!!!
!
INOSUKE? BUT WHERE?
UP HERE! UP HERE!
PASS THE CAT!!

HUCK 'IM!!
HUH?! HOW?!
TMP TMP TMP TMP TMP
HOP
NO WAY! THAT'S DAN—
WHA?! ROCKY?!
HOP
HOP
GAH!
FOMP
HE DID IT ALL BY HIMSELF!
WHOA!
YOU'RE SMART, ROCKY!!
INOSUKE!! I'LL SLOW SENSEI DOWN!
TRMBL
TRMBL TRMBL
TRMBL
HIDE ROCKY!
LEAVE IT TO ME!
PWIK
OKAY, KEEP PUSHING!

IS THIS THE RIGHT WAY?
YEAH! PHARMA-COLOGY CLUB STORAGE IS THIS WAY!
Make some room!
KLATR
MEOW!
ROCKY! NO!
HOP
AGH! HEY!
DA DA DA DA DA DA
GAH!
HOP
HOP
HUH? A CAT ?!
ACK!
WOBBL

!!
GASP
UH-OH!
INO-SUKE!!

AB
GR
HMF !!
SLAM
HIME-JIMA SEN-SEI !!
SLIP
OOPS!
!!

FWSH
TOK
...
DANGL
...
WHOA ...
SORRY, EVERY-BODY.
DOOM
DOOM

THIS IS ALL MY FAULT.
NO... WELL, YES.
APOLOGETIC
WE SHOULD PROBABLY BE MORE CAREFUL.
OH, THERE'S ZENITSU.
GRR GRR
TOOK YOU LONG ENOUGH.
THERE YOU ARE, HIMEJIMA SENSEI!!
YOU ALREADY FOUND TANJIRO AND INOSUKE?!
ZENITSU DIDN'T BRING YOU?
?
NOPE! I DID SOME-THING MORE IMPOR-TANT!!
HERE!
I FOUND ROCKY'S OWNERS!!

THANK YOU.

THEM?

TAMAYO SENSEI ...

... AND ...

YUSHIRO ?!

I SAW YOUR POSTERS.
IS THIS CAT YOURS?
WELL, UM...
CHACHA-MARU'S MY CAT.
RUB RUB
I BROUGHT HIM TO SCHOOL ONE TIME...
...AND HE TOOK A LIKING TO TAMAYO SENSEI...
...SO HE STARTED COMING EVERY DAY.
YUSHIRO
GINKGO CLASS
JUNIOR HIGH, SECOND-YEAR
I CAN'T KEEP HIM IN THE NURSE'S OFFICE, SO I LET HIM OUTSIDE.
Sorry for all the trouble.
OH, I SEE.
SO HIS NAME ISN'T ROCKY?
HMM...

WELL...
...I'M GLAD WE FOUND YOUR OWNER.

GRAH
HOW CAN YOU SAY THAT, YUSHIRO?!
JERK!
THAT CAT IS YOUR RESPONSI-BILITY!
GRAH
SHUT UP!!
GYAH
JUNIOR HIGH
HIGH SCHOOL
CHACHAMARU COMES BACK ON HIS OWN.
RATL
HE OPENS THE WINDOW HIMSELF AND HOPS IN!
Oh my!
HE OBVIOUSLY LIKES YOU...
...SO GO AHEAD AND KEEP PLAYING WITH HIM.
...!

LUCKY YOU, HIMEJIMA SENSEI!!
YEAH! FOR A MINUTE THERE...
...I THOUGHT YOU WERE GONNA CRY!!
YAAAY!!
O-OKAY ...
BUT, UM...
...CAN YOU?
GACK
THE SCHOOL'S RULES MIGHT POSE A BIT OF A PROBLEM...
THERE ISN'T ACTUALLY A RULE AGAINST THE CAT BEING HERE...
...SO IT'S NOT LIKE I CAN ACTUALLY FORBID IT.

REALLY ?!
SO WHY WERE YOU CHASING US AROUND?!
TOMIOKA WAS LENIENT (FOR ONCE).
AFTER THAT...
Wanna pet him?
No thanks.
...THE STUDENTS OFTEN SAW...
LOOK THIS WAY, SENSEI!
SNAP
...HIMEJIMA PLAYING WITH CHACHAMARU AT SCHOOL.
THAT SAID, REPLACING THE PHARMA-COLOGY CLUB'S SHELVES...
...COST QUITE A FEW BAGS OF DRIED SARDINES.
AND THAT'S WHY I KEEP TELLING YOU NOT TO RUN IN THE HALLS!

AWESOME ACADEMY

But no one has ever seen him angry.

CHAPTER 7: THE SECRET OF HOT SPRING EGGS

I MADE PLENTY OF CURRY...
...AND PUT IT IN THE FRIDGE...
...SO YOU CAN GET IT OUT AND WARM SOME UP EVERY DAY.
PAT
YOU ALREADY TOLD ME THAT!
WHY WOULD YOU WANNA...
...TAKE A TRIP TO SOME HOT SPRING RIGHT NOW ANYWAY?!
It's too hot!
INOSUKE HASHIBIRA
BAMBOO SHOOT CLASS
FIRST-YEAR
HOT SPRINGS IN THE SUMMER HAVE THEIR OWN CHARM.
SMILE
HISA
INOSUKE'S FOSTER PARENT
THERE'S ALSO CHILLED WATER-MELON...
...SO SHARE IT WITH YOUR FRIENDS.
I KNOW!!
TUNK

DON'T PASS OUT FROM THE HEAT, HISA!
DRINK PLENTY OF WATER!!
CHIRR CHIR
CHIRR CHIR
OKAY, I'LL TAKE GOOD CARE OF MYSELF.
GOOD LUCK WITH YOUR SUMMER CLASSES.
OH, RIGHT!

I'LL BRING YOU BACK SOME HOT SPRING EGGS.

UGH...

CHIR CHIR CHIR

So hot!

BETWEEN WORKING OUT AND SUMMER CLASSES ...

...THIS ISN'T A BREAK AT ALL!

ZENITSU AGATSUMA
BAMBOO SHOOT CLASS
FIRST-YEAR

AND ADDING HOMEWORK IN IS JUST CRUEL!

HM?

WHAT'S UP? WHY'RE YOU SO QUIET?

HEY, MONITSU?

WHAT ARE HOT SPRING EGGS?

CHIRR CHIR CHIR CHIRR

CHIR CHIR CHIRR CHIR CHIR

SKREE SKREE

BREAD! ♪ BREAD! ♪ KAMADO BAKERY! ♪
BAMBOO SHOOT CLASS FIRST-YEAR
CHATTER
Good morning!
CHATTER
TASTY FRESH-BAKED BREAD! ♪
GOBBLE IT UP! ♪
BREAKFAST? BREAD! SNACKS? BREAD!
THERE'S EVEN SOME FOR THE SLEEPY-HEAD! ♪
RATTL
GOOD MOOORNING !!
TANJIRO KAMADO
BAMBOO SHOOT CLASS
FIRST-YEAR
TANJIRO !!!
BOOM
OOF!
GYAAAAAH!

WHAT WAS THAT FOR, ZENITSU?!
NO QUESTIONS!!
JUST COME OUT BACK WITH ME!!
WHY?!
CLASS IS ABOUT TO—
TMP TMP TMP
FORGET ABOUT CLASS!

INOSUKE'S IN DANGER!!
HE IS?!

TMP TMP TMP TMP TMP TMP TMP
W-WHAT HAP-PENED?!
HISA'S TAKING A TRIP TO A HOT SPRING...

...AND SAID SHE'D BRING BACK HOT SPRING EGGS!
BUT INOSUKE DIDN'T KNOW WHAT THEY WERE...

"WHAT ARE HOT SPRING EGGS?"
...SO I TOLD HIM!!

HA HA HA

THEY'RE WHERE HOT SPRINGS COME FROM, DUH.

YOU DIG A HOLE, PLANT ONE...

...AND A HOT SPRING GUSHES OUT!!

SPLOOOSH

Here it comes!

HOT SPRING EGG

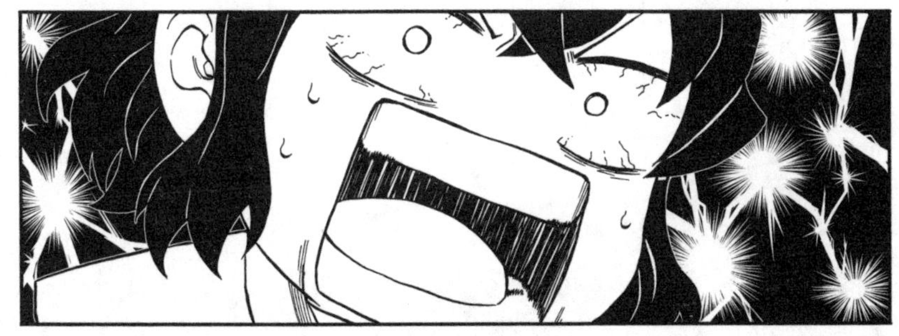

WHY'D YOU TELL HIM SUCH A STUPID LIE?!

—HOT SPRING EGGS (REAL)—
EGGS THAT HAVE BEEN BOILED SLOWLY AT LOW HEAT. YUM!

I DIDN'T THINK HE'D BELIEVE ME!

I THOUGHT IT'D BE MORE LIKE THIS!

AH HA HA!

Oh you!!!!

CHAT CHAT

!

WOOSH

GRAAAAAH!

?

GRAAAAH!

KIMETSU ACADEMY WESTERN GROUNDS

MOUNTAIN OUT BACK (FOOTHILLS)

CHIRR CHIRR

CHIRR CHIRR

CHIRR CHIRR CHIR

SHNK SHNK SHNK

WHEW!

THE BIGGER THE HOLE, THE BETTER, RIGHT?!

BY THE TIME HISA GETS BACK...
...I'LL HAVE A GIANT HOT SPRING ALL READY FOR HER!
SHNK
SHNK
HOT SPRING EGGS! HOT SPRING EGGS!
...

HE'S ACTUALLY DIGGING.
I THINK I'M GONNA CRY...
DOES HE EVEN HAVE A BRAIN?
YOU WERE THE ONE WHO LIED TO HIM!!

NOW WHAT, TANJIRO?
WHAT DO YOU MEAN?

LISTEN TO THIS, TANJIRO!!

WE'RE GONNA HAVE A HOT SPRING SOON!!

ULP

LISTEN, INOSUKE!!
IT'S ABOUT HOT SPRINGS!!
I KNOW!!
THEY'RE GOOD FOR YOUR HEALTH, RIGHT?
AFTER THIS ONE...
...I'LL GET STARTED ON ONE AT HOME!
IT'LL HELP SOOTHE HISA'S SORE BACK!
A GOOD SOAK EVERY DAY WILL CURE HER!
SHE WON'T EVEN NEED TO LEAVE THE HOUSE!
SHE'LL BE SO HAPPY!!
I'LL EVEN SHARE IT WITH YOU ALL TOO!!

AIN'T THAT GREAT?

BACK WHEN HANAKO WAS LITTLE...
TAKEO SAID A YOKAI INSIDE THE OVEN BAKES THE BREAD.
...TAKEO TOLD HER A BIG FIB.
HANAKO
THE KAMADO FAMILY'S SECOND-OLDEST DAUGHTER
TAKEO
THE KAMADO FAMILY'S SECOND-OLDEST SON

SHE WATCHED THE OVEN EVERY DAY, HOPING TO SEE THE YOKAI.
BA-BMP
BA-BMP
*TANJIRO'S FAMILY RUNS A BAKERY.
BUT WHEN I TOLD HER THE TRUTH...
Yokai don't actually exist.
SUN

PLIP
PLIP
PLIP

...SHE DIDN'T SPEAK TO ME FOR A WHOLE DAY!

FWMP
GUH...
THE TRUTH... BROKE HER HEART...
I'M A TERRIBLE BIG BROTHER!
WOBL
WOBL
HEY NOW! STOP WITH THE PITY PARTY!
THAT'S MY JOB!!
THE GUILT FROM THAT MOMENT IS KILLING ME!
AGH!
DON'T GO INTO THE LIGHT!!
I STILL NEED TO COPY YOUR HOME-WORK!!
WAAAAAAA
TANJIRO!! TANJIROO-OOOOO!!
HOW COULD THIS HAPPEN?!
OKAY, ENOUGH OF THAT.
Yeah.
WE GOTTA HELP INOSUKE.
IT WOULD BE NICE TO HAVE SOMEWHERE TO HYDRATE, THOUGH.

SHINOBU ?!
WHY'RE YOU THREE DITCHING SUMMER CLASSES?
SHINOBU KOCHO
MUGWORT CLASS
THIRD-YEAR
UH-OH!
BUT YOU'RE DITCHING TOO!!
MAYBE SHE CAN HELP US?
PSSST
PSSST
PSSST
PSSST
NO! SHE'LL CHIDE US FOR LYING!!
BUT ...!!
?
W- WE'RE, UM...
I'LL HAVE TO LIE FOR US!
AH!

HOT SPRING…
INO-SUKE…
EGGS…
DIGGING…
HISA…
WE'RE DIGGING AROUND HOPING WE CAN HIT A NATURAL HOT SPRING!!
AND INOSUKE'S SUPER STOKED!!
…
LIES BEGET MORE LIES, LEADING ONLY TO TRAGEDY.
WHAT A GREAT IDEA!
I'LL HELP YOU!
HUH ?!

BEFORE THEY BUILT THE SCHOOL ...

...THIS AREA WAS KNOWN FOR ITS HOT SPRINGS.

IT'S ENTIRELY POSSIBLE THERE COULD STILL BE SOME HIDING UNDER-GROUND.

?!

WAIT, REALLY ?!

YOU'VE NEVER HEARD OF...

...KIMETSU HOT SPRING?

KIMETSU HOT SPRING?!

WE COULD ACTUALLY SUCCEED?!

AND VISIT A HOT SPRING AT SCHOOL?!

THAT MEANS...

WHAT?! HOT SPRING EGGS ARE JUST A KIND OF FOOD?!
YOU DON'T HATCH HOT SPRINGS FROM THEM?!
SORRY!
HMPH!
FINE. I FORGIVE YOU...
...SINCE WE ACTUALLY DUG ONE UP!!
AHHH!
THIS FEELS GREAT!
WHO COULD COMPLAIN WHILE THEY'RE IN A HOT SPRING?
NEXT TIME, I'LL BRING HISA!!
YES!!

BAM!!

SHINOBU!! GUYS!

GRARAAAH!!!
KIMETSU HOT SPRING!!!
WHOA! YOU GUYS'RE HYPED!!
HECK YEAH!!
HOT SPRINGS'D SOLVE EVERY-THING!!
HUH? RIGHT!
IF WE HIT A REAL HOT SPRING...
...INOSUKE WON'T BE DISAP-POINTED!!
UWAAAAAAH
HOT SPRING!!
COMIN' THROUGH!!
♪
GRAAAAH!
SHUK SHUK

THREE HOURS LATER...

URGH

STILL NO HOT SPRING...

NOT EVEN A DROP...

HUFF

HUFF

MAYBE WE NEED MINING GEAR?

NO! WE CAN'T GIVE UP!!

GRRROWL

SHINOBU IS AN ANGEL!!
I ACTUALLY FEEL BAD ABOUT LYING TO HER!!
I ORDERED FOOD FROM THE DINER.
DELIVERY FOR KOCHO!
HINATSURU SENT FOOD!
GOTO
ENGLISH TEACHER
YOU DOIN' OKAY OUT HERE?
RUSTL
RUSTL
THANK YOU, GOTO SENSEI!
NO PROBLEM. BUT WHY'D YOU NEED FOUR—
OH.

SORRY. I NEEDED THEIR HELP WITH SOMETHING.

I'LL CLEAR IT LATER.

Really?

WELL, IF YOU SAY SO.

I'LL GO GET US SOME DRINKS!

CHIRR CHIRR CHIR CHIR

FEEL FREE TO EAT!

OKAY!

I FEEL BAD ABOUT THIS, BUT...

PSSST PSSST PSST

A HOT SPRING WILL MAKE HER HAPPY TOO!

NOW LET'S EAT!!

PWOK

UDON
GLEAM
THIS...
...LOOKS....
YUMMY!!
IT'S THE DINER'S TOP ITEM!
PERFECT FOR SUMMER!
COLD UDON WITH HOT SPRING EGG!!
UWAAAAAAH!
HOT SPRING EGG?
GYAAAAAH!

WHY ARE YOU SHOUTING?!
SHAKE NO SHAKE NO SHAKE NO
DID YOU SAY HOT SPRING EGG?!
HM?
YEAH! HOT SPRING EGG!
I LOVE 'EM. IN FACT, I SHOULD MAKE SOME LATER.
ALL IT TAKES ARE SOME NORMAL EGGS.
HM?
STOP RUNNING!!!
TMP TMP TMP TMP
YIIIIKES!

WE'RE SORRY, INOSUKE! WE CAN EXPLAIN!!
DON'T BOTHER!
GOTO JUST SAID THEY'RE NORMAL EGGS!!
NO WAY!
THEY'RE MORE THAN JUST NORMAL EGGS!!
?!
THEY'RE ...
FWP
...EXTRA-TASTY EGGS!
CRAZY CUTTING!!
YIKES!
ZEN-ITSU!!
THAT'S STILL JUST A FOOD!!
AH! THERE'S SHINOBU!

SENPAI! HELP US!

WSH

ARE YOU FIGHTING?

WSH

WE'LL TELL YOU EVERY-THING!

BLAH BLAH BLAH

OH, IS THAT WHAT HAPPENED?

AND THAT'S WHY YOU WERE RUNNING?

POUT

WHAT A SILLY LIE THAT WAS, ZENITSU!

YEAH... SORRY.

SORRY, INOSUKE.

Er...

DON'T BE MAD, OKAY?

...HOT SPRINGS OCCUR...

...WHEN GEOTHERMAL ACTIVITY HEATS GROUNDWATER.

HOT SPRING

AHH...

GROUNDWATER

HERE YOU GO!!

MAGMA

THEY'RE A NATURAL OCCUR-ANCE...

...THAT ONLY APPEAR IN CERTAIN PLACES.

THAT'S WHY THEY'RE SO VALUABLE.

THEY COULDN'T TELL YOU THE TRUTH...

...BECAUSE THEY DIDN'T WANT TO DISAPPOINT YOU.

SO HOW ABOUT FORGIVING THEM?

...

HMPH!

THANKS TO SHINOBU, I FORGIVE YOU.

INOSUKE!!

YOU'RE SO KIND!

WAHAHAHA

THE BEST!

WAHAHAHA

THANKS, SHINOBU!

HEY, SHINOBU!

YOU WANT MY HOT SPRING EGG?

YOU DON'T MIND?

Nah!

HISA'S BRINGING SOME HOME FOR ME!

TAKE THIS AS THANKS!

BUTTERFLY BRAND

SWUP

WHAT'S INSIDE?

BATH SALTS THE PHARMA-COLOGY CLUB MADE!

Club prez

THEY'RE GOOD FOR BACK PAIN!

REALLY?!

SHE HAD THAT PREPARED.

HUH?

SHE KNEW WE WERE LYING?!

No way!

I'LL BE GOING NOW.

ARE YOU GOING TO KEEP DIGGING?

NO. I'M LEAVING AFTER I EAT.

WHAT?!

DON'T YOU WANT TO FIND A HOT SPRING?

We'll help!

WHAT ABOUT KIMETSU HOT SPRING?

...

WHAT'RE YOU TALKING ABOUT?

YOU'LL NEVER FIND A HOT SPRING HERE!
KIMETSU HOT SPRING? SERI-OUSLY?
HUH?
A FEW DAYS LATER ...
...THE BOYS DISCOVERED THEIR HOLE...
...HAD BEEN TRANSFORMED INTO AN ARTIFICIAL POND WHERE THE PHARMACOLOGY CLUB COULD GROW HERBS.
SHE USED US...
...FOR FREE LABOR?
THEY DIDN'T FIGURE IT OUT...
...UNTIL AFTER THE POND WAS FINISHED.
YOKAN

DON'T LEAVE IT TO HER

CHAPTER 8: THE SQUEAL EQUATION

RMBL

KRAKOOM

SANEMI SHINAZUGAWA
MATH TEACHER

GENYA SHINAZUGAWA
CITRUS CLASS
FIRST-YEAR

THE NEXT DAY...
...AT KIMETSU ACADEMY'S SUMMER SESSION...
THAT'S ALL FOR TODAY.
SUMMER SESSION IS ALMOST OVER, SO GET READY FOR EXAMS.
TAP TAP
WHEW! IT'S ALMOST OVER!
BUT WE STILL HAVE EXAMS!
CHATTER CHATTER
I'M STAR-VING!
LET'S GRAB LUNCH AT AOZORA DINER!
CHATTER
SWP
TANJIRO KAMADO!
SLAAM

GAH!! PLEASE DON'T BEAT US UP!
HUH?
HEY, GENYA. WHAT'S UP?
WHY AM I THE ONLY ONE WHO'S SCARED?!
I HAVE A FAVOR TO ASK.
A O ZORA
YOU WANT US TO HELP YOU STUDY ?!
I NEED TO SCORE WELL ON EXAMS...
...THIS TIME AROUND.
WHAT ABOUT YOUR BROTHER? HE'S A MATH MONSTER!
SINE! COSINE! TANGENT! GRAH!
HE'S NOT A MONSTER!!
SNARF SNARF
GENYA SHINAZUGAWA IS SANEMI SHINAZUGAWA'S YOUNGER BROTHER.

I CAN'T ASK HIM!

BAM

WE HAD A FIGHT ABOUT MY GRADES!!

YOU CAN FIGHT HIM? RESPECT!

MNCH MNCH

WHAT HAPPENED?

MY FINAL EXAM SCORES SUCKED!

FLASH-BACK

RMMMMMMM

GOT THAT, GENYA?

IF YOU SCORE THIS BADLY AGAIN...

NEVER SCORE THIS LOW AGAIN!

YOU'RE NOT GETTING ...
...YOUR SUMMER FESTIVAL ...
...REDEMPTION VOUCHERS BACK!!
KRAKOOOM

Oh!
THAT'S THIS MONTH!
VOUCHERS?
FOR FREE GAMES AND STUFF?
YEAH...
URGH
...

WELL, BETTER KISS 'EM GOODBYE.
BUT I DON'T WANNA!!
NO WAY! I REFUSE!!
I'VE BEEN COLLECTING THOSE LIKE MAD!!
I HEAR YOU!
JUST CALM DOWN AND EAT!
WHAT WERE YOU PLANNING TO DO WITH 'EM?

ANYWAY, WE'LL HELP YOU.

RIGHT?

Well...

I DON'T MIND...

...BUT WHAT WAS YOUR RANK ON FINALS?

THIRTEENTH.

13/90

47TH

72ND

28TH

YAKINIKU RAMEN

SAUCE YAKISOBA

SALT YAKISOBA

NOM NOM

ARE YOU FOR REAL?!

NO WAY!

HOW THE HECK ARE WE SUPPOSED TO HELP YOU?!

SMARTYPANTS!

SALT

GYAH! YOU DON'T UNDERSTAND!

PIPE DOWN OVER THERE!!

JOLT

ACK!

SORRY, AOI!

AOI KANZAKI
PERSIMMON CLASS
SECOND-YEAR
(AOZORA DINER EMPLOYEE)

PSST PSST PSST

IT WAS MY MATH SCORES THAT WERE THE PROBLEM...

...SO I KNOW YOU CAN'T HELP ME!

PSST

JUST POINT ME AT SOMEONE WHO CAN!

WELL NOW I'M JUST OFFENDED.

NO GIRLS!
PICK A GUY!
SO...NOT KANAO OR SHINOBU?
KANAO
SHINOBU
NERVOUS AROUND GIRLS
YES, INOSUKE?
REFILL PLEASE.
HOW ABOUT MURATA?
SPARKL
HE'S AWAY AT SOCCER CAMP.
HMM
I KNOW!
IT DOESN'T HAVE TO BE AN *OLDER* STUDENT!
DING DONG
TOKITO

KLIK
YES?
TOKITO! WANNA HANG OUT WITH US?
WE DIDN'T COME TO HANG OUT ...
I SUSPECT SOME ULTERIOR MOTIVE.
MUICHIRO TOKITO
TARO CLASS
JUNIOR HIGH, SECOND-YEAR
YOU NEED HELP STUDYING?
WELL, GENYA DOES.
HEY!
PSST PSST
HE'S IN *JUNIOR HIGH!*
DOES HE KNOW HIGH SCHOOL STUFF?
DON'T WORRY! HE'S A PRODIGY!
HE MEMOR-IZES WHOLE TEXT-BOOKS!
RIGHT?
YEAH, I GUESS.

I'M FINE WITH HELPING...
...AS LONG AS YOU CALL ME "MR. TOKITO."
THIS KID'S ALREADY TICKING ME OFF!!
BUT GENYA'S TEST SCORES...
GENYA SHINAZUGAWA
MODERN LITERATURE
92
ENGLISH
GENYA SHINAZUGAWA
89
THEY'RE PRETTY GOOD!
Wow!
THE PROBLEM SEEMS TO BE THAT YOU RAN OUT OF TIME...
...AND MADE CARELESS MISTAKES BECAUSE YOU RUSHED.
Whoa!
WHAT YOU NEED TO DO...
...IS LEARN TO PAY MORE ATTENTION.
WHAT DO YOU MEAN?
DING DONG

HI! I'M HERE TO HANG OUT!!
KOTETSU ELEMENTARY SCHOOL, FOURTH-YEAR
KO-TETSU?!
HUH?! YOU'RE HERE, TANJIRO?!

BAM
WHAT THE HECK?!
SO COOL!!
THIS IS YORIICHI TYPE ZERO, A COMBAT DOLL!!
DOES IT MOVE?!
HERE, LEMME SHOW YOU.
HOLD THIS, ZENITSU.
WAIT. IT'S FOR COMBAT?
?
Water-melon?
TWIK
TWIK
TWIK
VEEN

CHOP
AAAIIIEEEE!!
TOO CLOSE!
ZEN-ITSU!!
HE'S GOT A GOOD SWING, RIGHT?
OH HECK NO!!
HOW'S THIS THING SUPPOSED TO HELP ME STUDY?!
I'VE GOT A BAD FEELING ABOUT THIS!
BUT IT'S PERFECT FOR BUILDING ...
... ACCURACY AND SPEED.
I'LL READ A QUESTION ...
...AND YOU ANSWER ...
...WHILE YORIICHI STANDS BEHIND YOU.
IF YOU'RE TOO SLOW OR YOU GET IT WRONG...

...THAT'LL BE YOUR HEAD.
* WATERMELON
THAT WOULD KILL ME!!

I'D BE DEAD!!!
IT'S GOOD FOR MOTI-VATION.

I'LL PROGRAM IT TO STOP FOR CORRECT ANSWERS.
TAK TAK TAK TAK TAK
YOU PROGRAM IT?!
THAT'S NOT JUST A DOLL, THEN!
AND WHAT'D YOU DO TO ITS HANDS?!

TOKITO, I THINK THIS IS A LITTLE TOO DANGER-OUS.
OH, OKAY.
WE'LL JUST HAVE IT SPLIT ANOTHER WATERMELON INSTEAD.
I have plenty.
FROM TETSUIDO
HOW IS THAT GONNA MOTIVATE ME?!

THAT'D BE TERRIBLE!!

I CAN'T LET THAT HAPPEN!!

GRAAAAAAH

IF THAT'S ALL IT TAKES, WHY'RE WE EVEN USING THAT THING?!

UM...

SHOULDN'T YOU THREE...

...BE STUDYING TOO?

HUH?

YOUR GRADES ARE WORSE THAN HIS, RIGHT?
DOESN'T THAT WORRY YOU?
POTTOK

YOU GET BAD GRADES WHEN YOU'RE LAZY.
HARSH

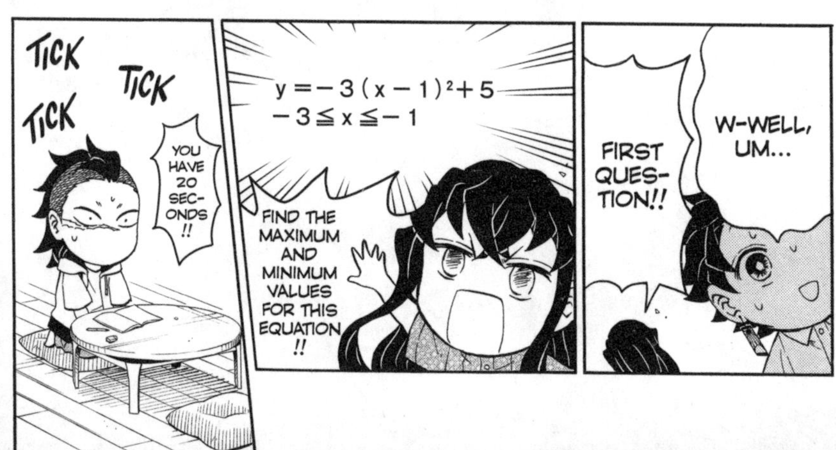
W-WELL, UM...
FIRST QUES-TION!!
y = − 3 (x − 1)² + 5
− 3 ≦ x ≦ − 1
FIND THE MAXIMUM AND MINIMUM VALUES FOR THIS EQUATION!!
TICK
TICK
TICK
YOU HAVE 20 SEC-ONDS!!

UM...X=-3 FOR A MINIMUM OF -43 AND X=-1 FOR A MAX OF -7!!!

CORRECT!

SHING

...

DURING SUMMER BREAK
IT IS WISE TO STUDY HARD
BUT WHO WOULD BOTHER?
—A SUMMER HAIKU BY THREE NINCOMPOOPS

TING

TING

GENYA'S DEDICATED!

BESIDES, YORIICHI IS BUSY WITH GENYA.

GAH!

CHOP

NO WORRIES! I'VE GOT ANOTHER ONE!!

I DIALED IT DOWN TO *GOOSE-EGG MODE.*

GYAH!

I'M NOT GETTING PUNCHED BY THAT THING!

NO WAY!

GYAHHH
YAHHH
C'MON, GUYS! STUDY!
NOOOOO!!
THUMP BUMP
KACHAK
I'M HOME!
QUIET DOWN OVER THERE!
UH-OH!!
OH, BIG BRO'S HOME!
CREAK
WHAT'S ALL THE EXCITE-MENT?
YUICHIRO TOKITO
GINKGO CLASS
JUNIOR HIGH, SECOND-YEAR
GRAAAAH
WELCOME HOME, YUICHIRO!!
CAN YOU HELP US STUDY?!
JOLT
?!

JUST USE YORIICHI TYPE ZERO!!
NAH, YUICHIRO WILL TEACH US!!
GETTING PUNCHED BY HIM WOULD HURT A LOT LESS!

...TANJIRO AND FRIENDS STUDIED...
CHOP
WATERMELOOON! AAAAGH!
...AT THE TOKITOS' HOUSE WHILE THEIR PARENTS WERE AWAY.
We're traveling!
Don't you understand this?
SIIIGH

I WAS HOPING I COULD SPEND THE NIGHT TONIGHT...

...SO ABOUT TOMORROW'S BREAD...

REALLY? THANKS, MOM!

RATL

PIP

TAKING A BREAK, GENYA?

YEAH.

WE'RE GONNA ORDER PIZZA.

KOTETSU'S RELATIVES RUN A PIZZA JOINT.

SOUNDS GREAT!!

Part-time delivery girl Mitsuru

BLEH...

DON'T WORRY! YOU'LL GET YOUR VOUCHERS BACK!!

LET'S ALL DO OUR BEST!!

Y-YEAH...

I KNOW THAT'S THE RIGHT ATTITUDE, BUT...

?

...I CAN'T BELIEVE THAT TOKITO...

...ALREADY KNOWS ALL THIS.

HE'S LIKE AN INFORMATION SPONGE.

YOU THINK SO?

...THEN MY BROTHER WOULDN'T GET MAD AT ME...

...FOR BEING A LOSER.

SPARKLE

HE MUST BE ASHAMED OF ME.

I'VE NEVER SEEN HIM SCOLD ANYONE ELSE FOR THEIR GRADES...

...BUT HE'S SUPER HARD ON YOU.

THAT'S A KIND OF FAVORITISM...

...ISN'T IT?

OKAY.
BUT FIRST...
...I'M GOING TO DO MY BEST.
Great!
QUIT CHATTING AND HELLLLLP !!!
TEST DAY...
CHATTER
CHATTER
CHATTER
EVERY-ONE GOT A TEST?
WE'RE STARTING IN 30 SECONDS!
FWP FWP
CHATTER CHATTER
BA-BMP BA-BMP
"THAT'S A KIND OF FAVORIT-ISM!"

AM I REALLY HIS FAVORITE?
IF THAT'S TRUE...
...THEN I GOTTA MEET HIS EXPECTATIONS.
WOW! YOU'RE NOT WASTING ANY WATERMELON!
YOUR BROTHER WILL SQUEAL IN DEFEAT!
YEAH...
...I'M GONNA DO IT!
MONTH
DAY
( )
FWIP
HE'LL SQUEAL...

BEGIN!!
9:00~
...AND ADMIT I KICKED BUTT!!
I'LL HAVE TO WORK QUICKLY AND CAREFULLY...
...SO I HAVE TIME TO CHECK MY WORK...
...AND MAKE SURE NO WATERMELON GETS WASTED!

KAW
STAFF
SKWIK
SKWIK
I'M LEAVING.
YOU GRADING TESTS?
SKWIK
SKWIK
YEAH.
AND THE SCORES ARE AWF—
SKWIK
SKWIK
...!
GENYA SHINAZUGAWA
SKWIK
GENYA SHINAZUGAWA
100
...
THOSE THREE SCORED HIGHER THAN USUAL?

A FEW DAYS LATER ...
... OUTSIDE THE SHINAZUGAWA RESIDENCE ...
A HUNDRED POINTS!!
I DIDN'T KNOW THAT WAS POSSIBLE!
IT'S NOT JUST A MYTH?!
Holy moly!
STOP GAWKING AT MY TEST!

D-
DID
HE...
...LEAVE
THEM HERE
FOR ME?
AND
WHAT'S
THIS?!
FREE
GENYA
FWP
MONEY?
FWP
DON'T BE A
TIGHTWAD.
SPEND THIS.
-SANEMI
"I BET
HE'LL EVEN
REWARD
YOU!!"
IT'S...
...COLD
HARD
CASH!!

CHATTER
CHATTER
GENYA! I WANT TAKOYAKI!
GAH! WHAT THE?!
YAKI-SOBA!
CANDIED APPLES!
SHAVED ICE!!
STOP DROOLING OVER MY VOUCHERS!!

AH HA HA!
AH HA HA!
Let's go!
SIGH...
WHY'RE YOU UP HERE, SANEMI?
LET'S GO TO THE FESTIVAL!

OKAY, OKAY...

YOU'RE GONNA TAKE ALL THE PRIZES AT THIS RATE!
WA HA HA
PLAYING AGAIN? THAT'S 300 YEN!
THE GUY RUNNING THE MARKSMANSHIP GAME IS THE ONE WHO REALLY WON HERE.

TOKITOS

FROM THEN ON, WHENEVER GENYA NEEDED HELP STUDYING...
...HE RELIED ON THE TOKITOS INSTEAD OF THE TANJIRO TRIO.
Huh?
What?
You got a prob-lem with us?
MU-ICHIRO'S CLASS...
IS TOKITO HERE?
HE JUST LEFT, BUT...
...HE MIGHT STILL BE IN THE HALL.
Oh, hey!
THERE HE IS!
TOKITO!
OLDER BROTHER: YUICHIRO
OH, YUICHIRO?
SORRY, I THOUGHT YOU WERE TOKITO.
I'M TOKITO TOO, Y'KNOW.
Whatcha need?

CHAPTER 9: THE KIMETSU ACADEMY NIGHT TOUR

IDEAS FOR THE SCHOOL'S SEVEN MYSTERIES?

YEAH! THE SCHOOL PAPER...

...PUT OUT A CALL FOR IDEAS!

IT SAYS, UM...

"LIKE OTHER SCHOOLS, KIMETSU ACADEMY SHOULD HAVE SEVEN MYSTERIOUS HAUNTINGS..."

"...SO WE'RE LOOKING FOR YOUR SPOOKY STORIES."

"ONCE WE HAVE SEVEN, WE'LL ANNOUNCE THE CHOSEN MYSTERIES."

Cool!

SPOOKY STORIES, HUH?

THE TERRIFYING BOAR-MAN UNDER THE FLOOR!!

SNORT

HUFF... HUFF... WHERE'S NEZUKO?

THE LEMON-HEADED LUNATIC STALKER!!

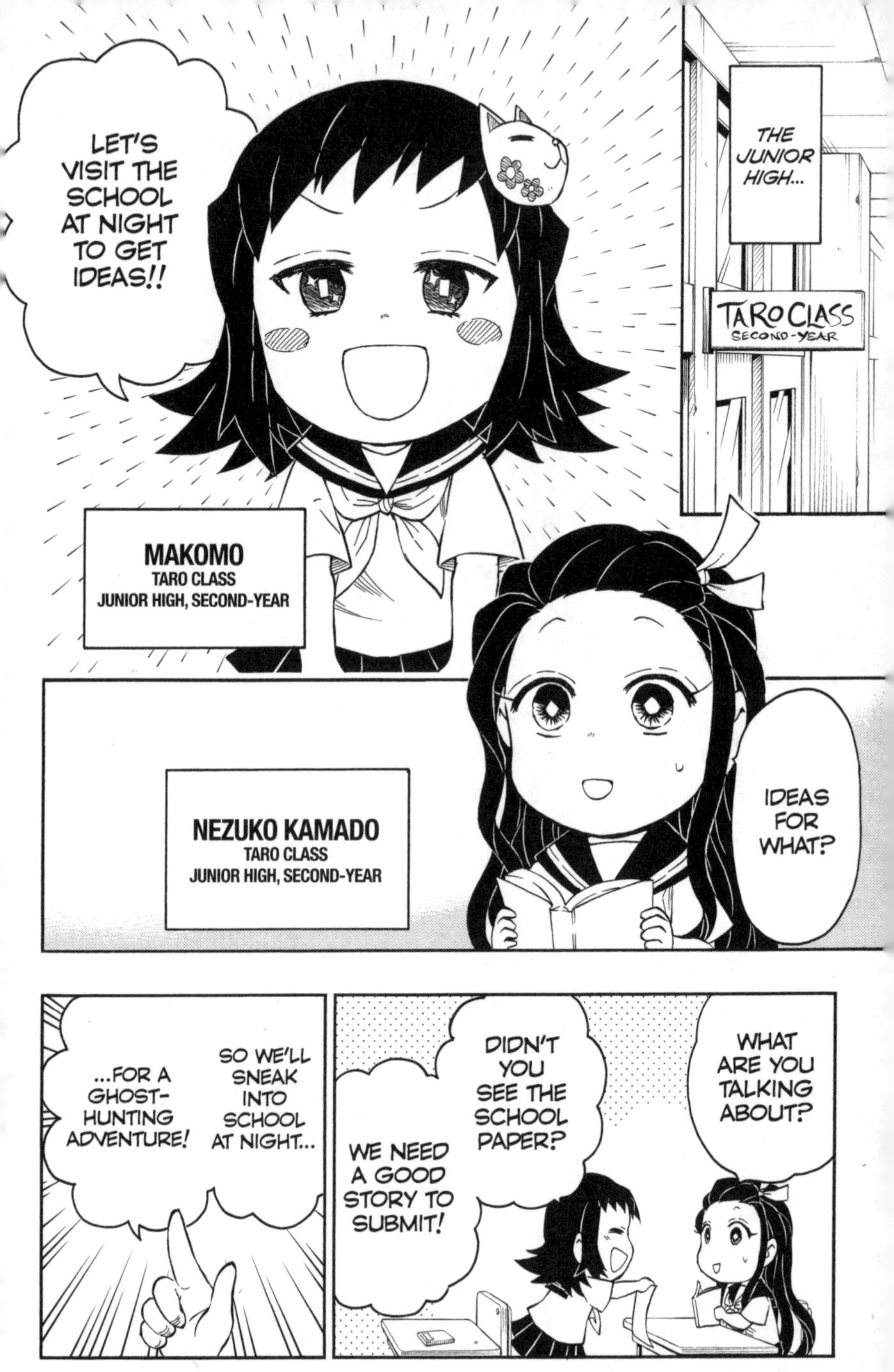

THE JUNIOR HIGH...

TARO CLASS
SECOND-YEAR

LET'S VISIT THE SCHOOL AT NIGHT TO GET IDEAS!!

MAKOMO
TARO CLASS
JUNIOR HIGH, SECOND-YEAR

IDEAS FOR WHAT?

NEZUKO KAMADO
TARO CLASS
JUNIOR HIGH, SECOND-YEAR

ADVEN-
TURE...
YAY

WAIT, WE CAN'T!
THERE'S NO WAY THE TEACHERS OR OUR PARENTS WOULD LET US!
THAT'S WHY WE'LL KEEP IT A SECRET!

TELL YOUR PARENTS YOU'RE SLEEPING OVER AT MY HOUSE!
BRING A FLASHLIGHT AND JUNK FOOD!
BEG BEG
BEG BEG
HMMM

WILL IT BE DANGER-OUS?
COULD BE!
THAT'S WHY WE'LL NEED A BODY-GUARD!

...
SABITO
TARO CLASS
JUNIOR HIGH,
SECOND-YEAR

BODY-GUARD

WELL, I GUESS I COULD...

YAHOO!!

WOO HOO

YAY! NOW WE'LL BE SAFE!!

NEZUKO AGREED TO GO.

BUT ISN'T THIS A BIT KIDDY FOR JUNIOR HIGH?

DON'T BE A SPOIL-SPORT!

YOU CAN INVITE A FRIEND IF YOU WANT!

UM...

...EXCUSE ME?

HM?

I FOUND THIS, AND IT HAD YOUR NAME...

...AND THIS CLASS WRITTEN ON IT.

SENJURO RENGOKU
AUTUMN LEAVES CLASS
JUNIOR HIGH, FIRST-YEAR

OH! MY HAND-KERCHIEF!

THANK YOU, SENJURO!

NO PROBLEM!

WELL, I'LL BE GOING NOW!

OH!

WAIT, SENJURO!

YES?

THAT NIGHT...

...AT THE JUNIOR HIGH...

WHOA...

THE SCHOOL FEELS...
...TOTALLY DIFFERENT AT NIGHT.

MAYBE THERE REALLY ARE GHOSTS!
BDMP BDMP
WELL, THE SCHOOL IS PRETTY OLD!
IF YOU SEE ONE, MAKE SURE YOU SNAP A PIC!

IF YOU'RE SCARED, GO HOME.

I CAN'T! THIS IS A TEST OF COURAGE FOR ME!

IT'LL HELP ME BE BRAVER!!

GWUP

THEN STOP CLINGING TO ME!

WALK ON YOUR OWN!!

Yikes! Why're you being so mean?

STOP BULLYING HIM, SABITO!

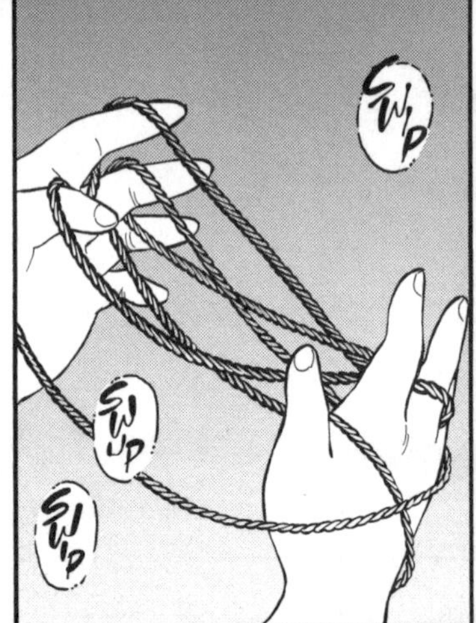
SWIP
SWIP
SWIP

SO! WHERE SHOULD WE LOOK?
MAYBE THE SCIENCE ROOM?
!
SHH!

WHAT'S WRONG, SABITO?
SOME-ONE'S IN THE CLASS-ROOM!
WHAT ?!

LOOK!
SWIP
SWIP

NO ONE ELSE SHOULD BE HERE THIS LATE!
TH-THEN IS THAT...
...A G-G-GHOST?
AH!
WHERE?

PIPE DOWN.

YEEEEEEK!

...MY CLASSMATE *RUI AYAKI!*

RUI AYAKI
AUTUMN LEAVES CLASS
JUNIOR HIGH, FIRST-YEAR

WHAT ARE YOU DOING HERE AT NIGHT?

I JUST DO THIS SOME-TIMES.

WHAT'RE *YOU* DOING HERE?

DO WHAT?

HANG OUT AT SCHOOL AT NIGHT.

BUT UNLIKE YOU, I DON'T MAKE A BUNCH OF NOISE.

I ENJOY PRACTICING CAT'S CRADLE...

...IN A NICE, QUIET, PEACEFUL ENVIRON-MENT!

VEEN

OOH, *ATTITUDE* MUCH?

YOU DON'T NEED TO BE SO GRUMPY.

CAN YOU MAKE TOKYO TOWER?!

...

SORRY. THEY'RE ALL IDIOTS.

IF YOU WANT SPOOKS...

...TRY THE HIGH SCHOOL.

SHALL WE CHECK IT OUT?
COME WITH US, RUI!
NO.

AW, C'MON!
WE'LL GIVE YOU SNACKS!
DON'T NEED 'EM.

...
FUMP
RUI'S KINDA WEIRD, HUH?
HE'S KIMETSU TOWN'S CAT'S CRADLE CHAMP!
NICE!
THE HIGH SCHOOL

I WAS ABLE TO LEAVE ONE OF THE JUNIOR HIGH'S WINDOWS UNLOCKED ...
...BUT THE HIGH SCHOOL'S GONNA BE LOCKED UP TIGHT.
Hmm...
I NEVER CONSID- ERED THAT!

LET'S START WITH THE THIRD FLOOR ...

...AND WORK OUR WAY DOWN.

IS IT TOO LATE...

...TO WORRY ABOUT WHETHER WE COULD GET IN TROUBLE FOR THIS?

TAK

YEAH. THAT'S THE ACTUAL SCARY THING HERE.

TAK

RELAX!

PSHHH

ANYWAY, THERE MUST BE SOMETHING HERE! RUI SAID SO!

HM?

PSHHHHHH

PWUF

PWUF

PSHOOO

DID YOU HEAR THAT?

PSHOOO

PSHHH

IT'S KINDA CREEPY.

YEAH, LIKE WEIRD BREATHING...

SHIVR

HWAAH
PSHOO
IT'S COMING FROM UPSTAIRS.
RIGHT! LET'S CHECK IT OUT!
HUH?!! NO, WAIT!
NO FEAR!!
LET'S JUST GO HOME!!
WE'LL DIE IF WE GO LOOKING FOR IT! I KNOW IT!
IT'S JUST LIKE IN THE MOVIES!!
IT'S THE CURIOUS ONES WHO DIE FIRST!!!
YOU'RE A SCAREDY-CAT WHO WATCHES HORROR MOVIES?
PSHOO
IT'S COMING FROM THE HOME EC ROOM!!
PWUF
HURRY!
I WOULDN'T IF I WERE YOU...
...!
HWAAAH
PEEK
IT'S...
...THERE!!
PSHHHH

PSHHH
PING! ♫
YOUR RICE IS READY! ♫
A
SEN-JURO?!
BIG BROTHER?!!
RENGOKU SENSEI?!
EEEEE

FWOO
OH DEAR...
KYOJURO RENGOKU
HISTORY TEACHER
(SENJURO'S OLDER BROTHER)

WHAT ARE YOU DOING HERE AT THIS HOUR?!
IS HE GONNA LECTURE US?!
YOU'RE HERE TOO, BIG BRO...

HERE FOR A LATE-NIGHT SNACK?
YEP!! I'VE GOT THE MUNCHIES!
SKIR
SKIR
BUT WHY SNACK AT SCHOOL?
CAN I TAKE A PIC FOR THE SCHOOL PAPER?
The steamy specter...
...who reaps rice in the home ec room!
PLEASE DON'T, YOUNG MAN!

THAT'D GIVE PEOPLE THE WRONG IDEA!!
AFTER ALL, I DIDN'T JUST SNEAK IN HERE AT NIGHT TO MAKE RICE!!
I'M A GIRL...
THAT'S A... RELIEF.
I'M THE NIGHT GUARD!!
THE WHAT?
OH. HE PATROLS THE GROUNDS OVERNIGHT.
YEP!
MOST SCHOOLS DON'T DO THIS ANYMORE!
BUT KIMETSU ACADEMY HAS A GOOD REASON TO!
SO IT'S A TRADITION!

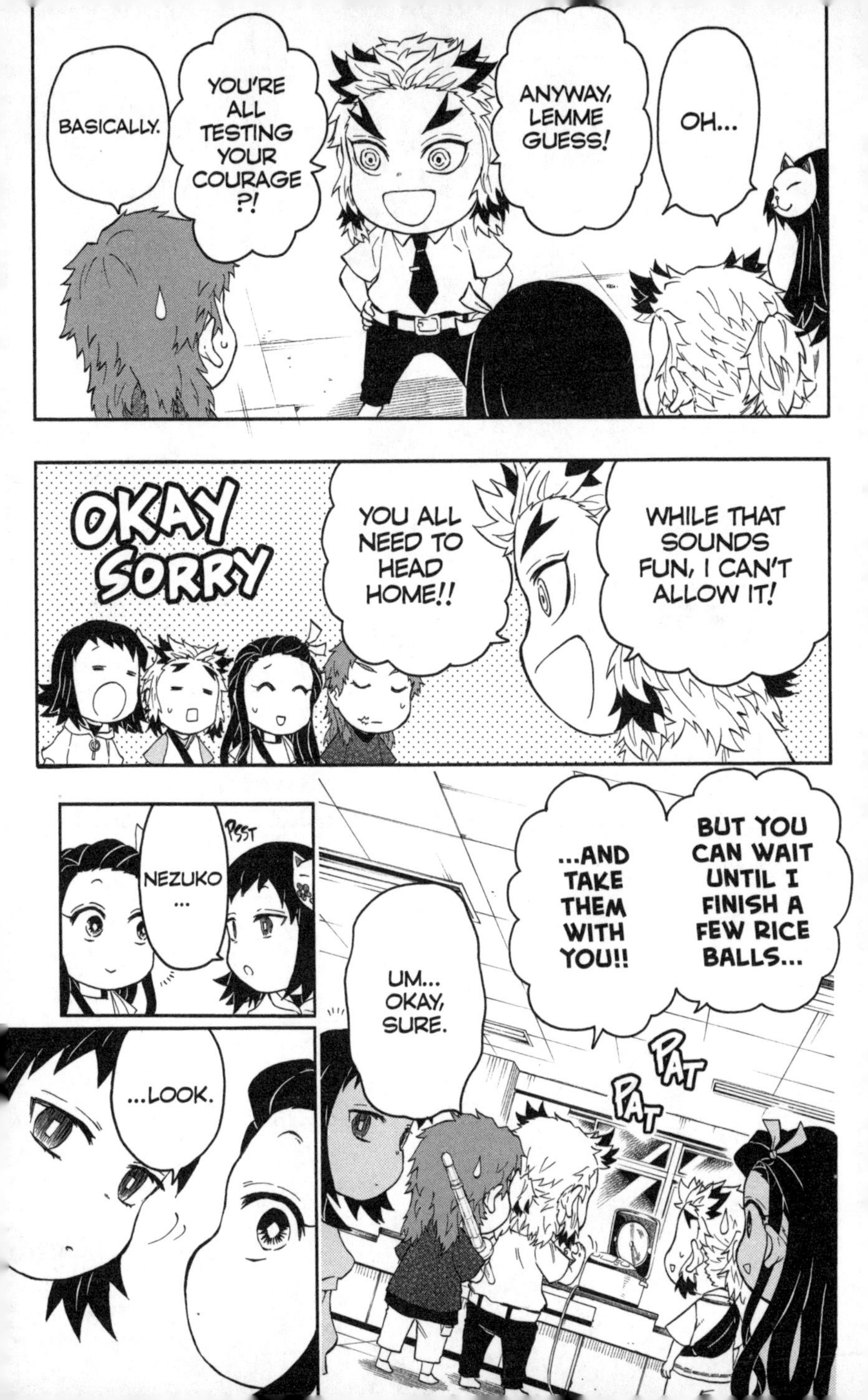

WHILE THAT SOUNDS FUN, I CAN'T ALLOW IT!
YOU ALL NEED TO HEAD HOME!!
OKAY SORRY

BUT YOU CAN WAIT UNTIL I FINISH A FEW RICE BALLS...
...AND TAKE THEM WITH YOU!!
UM... OKAY, SURE.
PAT
PAT

PSST
NEZUKO...

...LOOK.

THOSE GHOSTLY HANDS ARE BECKONING US...

THERE! ALL FINISHED!!

I TRIED COOKING THE INGREDIENTS INTO THE RICE THIS TIME!

"THIS TIME"?

DO YOU DO THIS OFTEN?

UH-OH...

WHERE'D THE GIRLS GO?

BIOLOGY
HYO HYO!
YOU GALS HAVE FALLEN INTO MY HANDS!
TREMBLE IN FEAR!!
FOR I AM KIMETSU ACADEMY'S GREATEST HORROR!!
I'LL DRAG YOU INTO THIS FINE VASE OF MINE!!
BAM
GYOKKO
SCHOOL HORROR
*EYES: UPPER/FIVE
EEP!
A MONSTER!!!
HYO HYO!
YES! TREMBLE IN FEAR!!

MAY WE TAKE A SELFIE WITH YOU?!
IS THE FLASH ON?
ARE MY BANGS ALL RIGHT?
EVERY-ONE, LOOK AT THE CAMERA!
SAY, "CHEESE"! ☆
CLICK☆
NO MORE OF THAT!!!
WHOOPS. HE'S MAD.
DON'T TAKE ME LIGHTLY!!
LURK
?!

TRMBL
TRMBL
HOW HORRIBLE, HOW HORRIBLE ...
STUDENTS ENJOYING THEIR YOUTH!
HANTENGU
SCHOOL HORROR
GIVE ME YOUR YOUTH!
OR OTHER VALU-ABLES!
BONK
GEH!
SKF
ARE YOU TWO ALL RIGHT?
SABITO!
YIKES!
OUCH!
HOLD THAT POSE WHILE I SNAP A PIC!
RIGHT NOW?! REALLY?!
WHAT'S WITH THIS SCHOOL?!
TL
RIN!
PA
FWIP

PYO!
TO!
SHA!
KAI!
?!
JIN!
RETSU!
ZAI!
ZEN!
SWAP
?!
FOUL SPIRITS, BEGONE !!
KRAKL
ONKIRIKIRI AKKIMES-SATSU SOWAKA!!
YIKES

GYAAAAAAAAAH!
KRAKL
KRAKL
...
SWOO

WHAT...
...THE HECK?!?
WHAT JUST HAPPENED?
OH!
FWIP
THOSE CREEPS ALWAYS SHOW UP HERE AT NIGHT.
THE NIGHT GUARD'S JOB IS TO ERASE 'EM!!
LIKE SCRIBBLES ON A BLACKBOARD?!

YOU CAN DO EXORCISMS?!
ALL THE HIGH SCHOOL TEACHERS CAN!!
THEY ALL CAN?!
R-REALLY?!
ALL OF THEM?!
YOU ALL JUST GO AROUND EXORCISING GHOSTS AND GHOULS?!
GYAAAH
YEP! THAT'S RIGHT!
TO BE HONEST, THOUGH ...
...ANYONE CAN SLAP ON A SEAL ON SOME SPOOKS!
And chant somethin'!
THESE SEALS ARE THAT POWERFUL?
THE SHOCKING TRUTH COMES OUT.
I had no idea.
YEAH, I CAN'T SUBMIT THAT.

...''THE CREEPY OLD BABY GUY'' AND ''THE GUY IN A POT''...

...WERE ENSHRINED AS TWO OF THE SCHOOL'S SEVEN MYSTERIES.

THEY KEPT THE NIGHT GUARD SECRET, THOUGH.

GWOOOO
...WHAT ARE YOU COPYING?
OH, THAT?
VRRR
VRRR
TEE HEE!
IT BEATS WRITING THEM BY HAND!
Right?
??
THE SOURCE OF THE SEALS WAS CLOSE AT HAND.

LIFE IN TARO CLASS

CHAPTER 10: LOVE AND SNAKES

IT HAPPENED ONE AUTUMN DAY...
LOOK OVER THERE.
TANJIRO KAMADO
BAMBOO SHOOT CLASS
FIRST-YEAR
ZENITSU AGATSUMA
BAMBOO SHOOT CLASS
FIRST-YEAR
PACE
PACE
SIGH
MITSURI KANROJI
UNIVERSITY STUDENT
ISN'T THAT THE PIZZA DELIVERY GIRL?
YEAH!
SHE VISITS AOZORA DINER A LOT TOO!

WHATCHA HANGIN' AROUND HERE FOR?!

SHOUT

D'YOU NEED SOMETHIN'?!

GASP

KYAH!

I BET I LOOK SUSPICIOUS, HUH?!

BUT I GRAD-UATED FROM HERE!

Oh!

YOU DID?

WANT US TO GET SOME-ONE FOR YOU?

NO, I'M FINE. THANKS.

WHAT I REALLY NEED...

...IS A CROW TO DELIVER THIS LETTER FOR ME.

IS THAT A LOVE LETTER?!
THIS BEAUTY IS SENDING A LOVE LETTER...
BDMP BDMP
...TO SOMEONE HERE AT SCHOOL?!
WANT US TO DELIVER IT FOR YOU?
REALLY?! YOU'D DO THAT?!
SURE!
THANKS SO MUCH!!
OKAY, HERE'S THE LETTER!

NO FREAKING WAY...

WELL, I GUESS HE'S POPULAR!
NOT A CHANCE!
HE'S A GLOOMY AND ANNOYING SNAKE!!
NAG NAG
Oh, you forgot your homework?
Then why even bother coming?!

I CAN'T BELIEVE IT!!
HE BEAT ME!!
ROMANCE ISN'T A COMPETITION! BE STRONG, ZENITSU!
FINE, WHATEVER. BUT...

IT'S FOR...
CHEMISTRY
...OBANAI IGURO?! OUR CHEMISTRY TEACHER?!

...THAT GUY AND KANROJI?
I BET SHE'LL DUMP HIM!
HM?
AFTER ALL...

...HE'S BASICALLY ALLERGIC TO WOMEN!
WOMAN
WOMAN
HIS HEART POUNDS AND HE SWEATS BUCKETS!
HE'LL PROBABLY FROTH AT THE MOUTH AND COLLAPSE!
Mask
Ward against women? Kaburamaru (snake)
SO MAYBE IT'D BE BEST IF WE DIDN'T DELIVER THIS.
WELL, IT'S NOT OUR DECISION.
ANYWAY, UM...
...
OBANAI IGURO
CHEMISTRY TEACHER

...THIS LETTER IS FOR YOU.

HISSS

Keep that away from me!

CHOMP

HWIP

GOOD.

GRIP

THANK YOU FOR DELIVERING IT.

?!!

Y-YOU WERE EXPECTING THAT?!
WHAT ?!
DOES SHE SEND YOU LOTS OF LETTERS?!
HUH?! DO YOU GET LOTS FROM HER?!
NONE OF YOUR BUSINESS!
LOVE LETTERS ARE PRIVATE!!
FORGET THIS EVER HAPPENED!!
SILENCE
UM... WHAT'D YOU TWO DO?
WE...
...SHOULDN'T HAVE GOTTEN INVOLVED.
?
ONE WEEK LATER...
BOOM
GYAAH

DOOM
HELP ME FIND A PRESENT FOR KANROJI.
?
I'M TALKING TO YOU TWO.

I WOULD RATHER NOT INVOLVE STUDENTS BUT...
...YOU'RE THE ONLY ONES I CAN TRUST WHO KNOW ABOUT THIS.

KANROJI WENT TO SCHOOL HERE, RIGHT?
WHY NOT ASK THE OTHER TEACHERS?
EVERYONE WHO KNOWS HER RECOMMENDED FOOD.
*IGURO DIDN'T START WORKING HERE UNTIL AFTER SHE GRADUATED.

DOES HE...NOT HAVE ANY NON-WORK FRIENDS HE COULD ASK?
WHAT'S WITH THE LOOK?
WE ALWAYS GO OUT TO EAT, SO I NEED SOMETHING BESIDES FOOD!

WHY SHOULD I CARE...
...ABOUT SOME OTHER GUY'S DATE GOING WELL?
SURE! I'D BE HAPPY TO!!
WHAT ?!

REALLY?

YEAH!

ZENITSU WILL HELP TOO!!

I WILL ...?

WHAT'S THE PAY LIKE?

HE DOESN'T HAVE TO PAY US!!

THEN WHY SHOULD I— *UGH!*

HMM...

I *SHOULD* REPAY YOU SOMEHOW ...

HOW ABOUT I BUY YOU LUNCH?

But keep it secret.

RATTL

I'LL TREAT YOU TO WHATEVER YOU WANT.

FREE LUNCH? I'M IN!!

NO!!!

INOSUKE HASHIBIRA
BAMBOO SHOOT CLASS
FIRST-YEAR

THIS WEEKEND, RIGHT?!
NO ONE INVITED—
INOSUKE!!
JOLT
YOU PROMISED TO HELP OUT AT THE DINER THIS WEEKEND!!
TO PAY FOR ALL THE BROKEN DISHES!!
AOI KANZAKI
PERSIMMON CLASS
SECOND-YEAR
ULP! AOI...
YOU SHOULD KEEP YOUR PROMISE.
OR YOU'LL LOSE FREE REFILLS.
BUT... FOOD...
YOU CAN HAVE A FREE TEMPURA BOWL!
SORRY. SEE YA, DUDES.
WHY'D YOU EVEN BOTHER SHOWING UP?
AND SO THE MATTER WAS SETTLED.

BAM

THAT WEEK-END...

...AT THE TRAIN STATION...

さぎりやま駅
Sagiriyama Station

GACK

SEN-SEI!!

I'VE GOTTA SAY, I HATE SEEING TEACHERS ON THE WEEKEND!!

KEEP IT TO YOURSELF.

UM, SEN-SEI?

WE DON'T REALLY KNOW WHAT COLLEGE GIRLS LIKE.

HONEY, HONEY, BUZZ!
HM?
IT'S IGURO!!!
AND HE'S WITH THE BOYS WHO DELIVERED MY LETTER!!
Good rentals
KANROJI'S IMAGINATION
HIS STUDENTS MUST WORSHIP HIM!!
Wee hee hee!
Ah ha ha!
IGURO IS SO COOL!
I'VE ALWAYS WANTED TO SEE HIM TEACH...
...BUT WHY ON THE WEEK-END?
SNEAK

Cute SHOP

OH!

AN ACCES-SORY SHOP?

T FOR YOU

US ON 2F →

COULD HE BE...

KYAH!!

...BUYING A PRESENT FOR ME?!!

SHE FIGURED IT OUT INSTANTLY!

CAN I HELP YOU?
Welcome!
A SALES LADY!
WHAT DO WE DO?!
I'M TOO EMBARRASSED TO ASK!!
TUMP
WE'RE TRYING TO PICK OUT A GIFT FOR A UNIVERSITY STUDENT!!!

THEY'RE PRETTY!!
LET ME KNOW IF YOU NEED MORE HELP!
THANKS A LOT!!

...

PFFF
!!!

SHE SNICKERED AT YOU!!!
IT'S ONLY A LITTLE EMBARRAS-SING TO ASK.
YES, BUT SENSEI SHOULDA DONE IT!!

WHERE IS HE, ANYWAY?!
FWIP
FOR YOU.

YOU'RE PRETENDING WE'RE STRANGERS ?!!
BOOOOM
GUH!
WE'RE HERE BECAUSE OF YOU!!

HOW ABOUT A HAIR ORNAMENT, SENSEI?
HMM...
I BET THIS ONE'D LOOK GOOD ON KANROJI.

YES, IT WOULD ...

THAT SETTLES IT! NOW—
HOWEVER ...

SHE'LL BE WEARING IT AROUND OTHER PEOPLE, SO IT'S MORE IMPORTANT...
...WHETHER IT'S TO HER TASTE.
I WOULDN'T WANT HER TO FEEL OBLIGATED TO WEAR SOMETHING SHE DIDN'T LIKE.

GWOOOOOOO

IS SHOP-PING FOR GIRLS REALLY THAT HARD?

What a pain!

IF HE ASKED FOR OUR HELP...

...HE MUST BE SERIOUS ABOUT THIS.

Not this one...

Not this one either...

Nope...

No...

IT'S PAST NOON.

SHALL WE BREAK FOR LUNCH?

ARE YOU EVEN TRYING?!

WE HAVEN'T MADE ANY PROGRESS ALL MORNING!

I'LL DECIDE THIS AFTERNOON.

FAMILY RESTAURANT

Welcome!

FAMILY RESTAURANT

DOES THIS PLACE WORK FOR YOU?

YEAH! THE MENU'S GOT VARIETY!

HONESTLY, I PREFER FINER DINING...

Tastes great!
Yeah!
Yum!
Mm-mm!
...
HEY, SEN-SEI!
CAN WE ORDER PARFAITS TOO?!
SURE.
Heh...
ORDER WHATEVER YOU WANT.
PAPING
WOW! IGURO IN ACTION!
I WONDER WHAT THEY'RE TALKING ABOUT.
NOM NOM NOM NOM NOM
NOM NOM NOM
HE'S BEING SO NICE IT'S ACTUALLY KINDA CREEPY.
BVVT BVVT

HELLO? THIS IS KANROJI.
OH! HI, TECCHIN!!*
*HER BOSS
AHEM, MITSURI?
I TAKE IT YOU'VE FORGOT-TEN?
?
ABOUT WHAT?
YOUR SHIFT THIS AFTERNOON! ♡
OMIGOSH! S-SORRY! I GOT DISTRACTED!
FWOOOOSH
THAT'S ALL RIGHT.
TAKE CARE ON THE WAY HERE.
WELL, WHAT'S NEXT?
HMM...
AH HA HA HA!
KYA HA HA HA!
NO WAY!
?

REALLY, HEBIKO?!

YEAH!! MY BOO BOUGHT THIS BAG FOR ME!!

NO WAY! IT'S HIDEOUS!

GUY'S GOT NO FASHION SENSE! WA HA HA!

WA HA HA BWA HA HA

...!!

HE EVEN SAID HE SPENT *ALL DAY* PICKING IT OUT!!

EW! CREEPY!!

TITTER TITTER GIGGLE GIGGLE GUFFAW

DO THEY HAVE TO BE...

...SO LOUD?

UM, IGURO SENSEI?

DON'T WORRY.

HM?

I'M FINE.

KANROJI ISN'T LIKE THAT.

SSIP

WELL, IF YOU'RE SURE...

Thanks for coming in!
FAMILY RESTAURANT

...

BUT... AM I CREEPY TOO?
HM...
NO, NOT AT ALL!!!

YOU'RE DOING FINE!!
NO...
...I'M OVER-THINKING THINGS.
GLASSES

I love me...
...some eats!
WHAT KANROJI LIKES IS OBVIOUS...
...SO I SHOULD GET HER SOMETHING SWEET.

OFF-SEASON, LIMITED-QUANTITY, *HYPER SAKURA MOCHI!*

THIS PLACE IS ADVERTISING A GORGEOUS JAPANESE CONFECTION!!

AHA!

A TREAT, HUH?

CHATTER CHATTER CHATTER

LET'S GO STRAIGHT THERE!!

KANROJI DOES LIKE SAKURA MOCHI.

DADOOM

JAPANESE SWEETS

AUTUMN DUMPLINGS

OHAGI

CHESTNUT DAIFUKU

MONAKA

MUGWORT MOCHI

BEAN MOCHI

HYPER SAKURA MOCHI

...!!

SHF
SHF
OH NO!
THE LINE'S GETTING EVEN LONGER!
THEY'RE GONNA RUN OUT!
DASH
WE'LL GET IN LINE FOR YOU, SENSEI!!
YOU CAN DO IT, TEACH!
HUFF HUFF
WE'RE ALMOST THERE!
ONLY 20 MORE PEOPLE!
JUST TEN MORE!
FIVE!
WE'RE NEXT!!
SWP
CLMP
NO...
...I HAVE TO DO THIS MYSELF!!

THE HYPER SAKURA MOCHI JUST SOLD OUT!!
TUNK
SOLD OUT
KAW KAW
WE WERE SO CLOSE...
YOUR BRAVERY WAS IMPRESSIVE, SENSEI!!
YOU JUST NEEDED TO BE BRAVER SOONER!
YES, YOU'RE RIGHT.
I HAVE FAILED.
Well he's bummed.

I COULD BARELY LINE UP TO BUY MOCHI.

SNAKE SCARF
SHE GAVE ME A BIRTHDAY PRESENT THE OTHER DAY.

SHE GIVES ME SO MUCH...
...SO I WANTED TO DO THE SAME FOR HER.
...

SWIP
OH WELL. LET'S GO HOME.
HUH ?!
SORRY FOR BOTHERING YOU TWO WITH THIS.

BUT WHAT ABOUT A PRESENT ?!
THIS ISN'T A SPECIAL OCCASION.
I'LL GET HER SOMETHING SOME OTHER TIME.

IT WAS JUST SOMETHING I WANTED TO DO.

"IT WAS TASTY!"
"THANKS SO MUCH, ZENITSU!"

YOU HAVE TO GIVE HER A PRESENT !!!

Z-ZEN-ITSU?

MOPING DOESN'T SOLVE ANYTHING!

YOU'VE GOTTA SHOW YOUR FEELINGS !!

BECAUSE PRESENTS ...

...ARE GOOD FOR BOTH THE GIVER AND THE RECEIVER!!

EVEN IF IT'S JUST FOR YOU, YOU'VE GOT TO GIVE HER A PRESENT!!

FORGET SHE'S A COLLEGE GIRL!
JUST BUY SOMETHING FOR *HER*!!
YOU KNOW HER BETTER THAN ANYONE!
YOU REALLY THINK SO?
HURRY! BEFORE THE SHOPS CLOSE!
ALSO, TRY SHOPPING ONLINE NEXT TIME!
YOU'RE TOO OLD-FASHIONED!
MEAN-WHILE...
HERE'S AN ACORN FOR YOU, AOI!
UH, THANKS?
ON A LATER DATE...
AH, THAT WAS DELICIOUS!

I LOVE HAVING DINNER WITH YOU!!
OH?
BY THE WAY...
...I BROUGHT SOMETHING FOR YOU.
RUSTL

AND THEY'VE GOT—!
BIG HAND CAT IS AN ORIGINAL CHARACTER...
...THAT KANROJI DESIGNED AS AN ART STUDENT.
Lookie, Iguro!
I SEARCHED ONLINE FOR A SHOP...
...THAT WOULD EMBROIDER THEM BASED ON YOUR ILLUSTRATION.
I WANTED TO DO IT MYSELF, BUT IT WAS TOO DIFFICULT.
Here, Sensei!!
This place'll do it!!
I ALSO HAD THEM EMBROIDER...
...SOMETHING FOR ME.
SHF

A HANDKERCHIEF...
FWIP
...TO MATCH YOUR SOCKS.
...
PLIP
?!

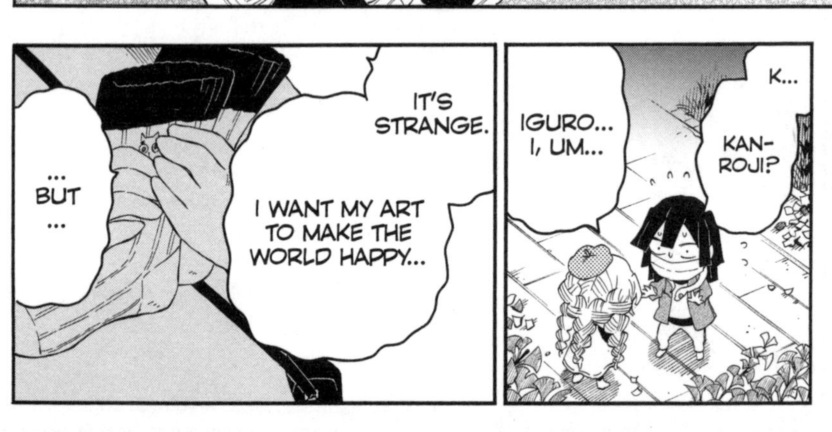

...RIGHT NOW...
...IT'S MAKING ME THE HAPPIEST OF ALL!
OH...
THAT'S GOOD.
I'M GLAD.
IGURO...
...WOULD GO ON TO BE MUCH KINDER TO TANJIRO AND ZENITSU.
JUST KIDDING!
NO NAP-PING IN CLASS!
BUT NOW WHEN THEY SEE...
...A CROW CARRYING A LOVE LETTER...
...THEY CAN'T HELP BUT SMILE.

CHAPTER 10 DELETED SCENES
USELESS TEACHERS

Kanroji in high school

BUY HER A FRUIT FIELD! SHE'D LOVE THAT!
YOU COULD GROW FLOWERS THERE! HOW ROMAN-TIC!
KOCHO SENSEI'S IDEA WAS ROMANTIC (BUT UN-REALISTIC.)

COLLEGE KIDS ARE POOR!!
SO TREAT HER TO A FINE MEAL!!
UZUI WENT FOR STEREO-TYPES.

SHE'LL LIKE ANYTHING YOU GET HER.
GOTO PLAYED IT CASUAL.
A GRIND-STONE.
HAGANE-ZUKA SENSEI RECOM-MENDED THINGS HE WANTS.

SHE CAN'T BUY FROM THE SCHOOL KIOSK ANYMORE...
...SO STUFF HER WITH FOOD.
KYOGAI SENSEI WAS THOUGHT-FUL.

HOW ABOUT A BAG OF RICE?!
DESPITE BEING HER FORMER TEACHER, RENGOKU WAS STILL RENGOKU.

HE DIDN'T BOTHER ASKING TOMIOKA SENSEI.

WHICH ONLY LEFT...
...
THAT EXPLAINS IT.

VOLUME 2 (END)

EXIT
くもとり
KUMOTORI
THIS IS TAMIO ENMU.
TANJIRO ALWAYS CATCHES HIM MIS-BEHAVING ON THE TRAIN.*
HE'S A TRAIN GEEK WITH A CRIMINAL HABIT.
*SEE VOL. 1, CHAPTER 1.
♪
*EYES: LOWER ONE
BONUS CHAPTER: KUMOTORI STATION, 7:30 A.M.
TMP TMP
くもとり
KUMOTORI
...
TMP
TMP
TMP

FOMP

GWOOOOOOO

WHY DID YOU SIT NEXT TO ME?

SO I CAN NAB YOU WHEN YOU MOON PEOPLE!

HOW RUDE!

YOU MAKE ME SOUND LIKE A FLASHER!

WELL, AREN'T YOU?

YES, I AM.

CLOTHES COME BETWEEN ME AND THE TRAIN ...
...AND I CAN'T STAND IT.
BUT WHEN I STRIP DOWN...
I WEAR...
YAY
...THE TRAIN!!!
MAKE SENSE?
NO. BUY A TRAIN AND DO IT AT HOME.
THAT'S A BIT COSTLY.
BESIDES, OTHER PASSEN-GERS ARE PART OF THE EXPERIENCE.
SORRY. I JUST DON'T GET IT.
...

WHY CAN'T I DISROBE ON THE TRAIN?

BECAUSE OF BOX LUNCHES!!

BAM

A TRAIN IS NOW ARRIVING AT...
THANKS FOR THE ADVICE.
HERE. HAVE A YUZU JELLY DRINK!
Shake it first!
OH! THANKS!
FARE-WELL NOW!
RRRING
PANTS
THE END!

CIVICS

Welcome to volume 2! Thanks for reading! Just like with volume 1, this was only possible through the efforts of a lot of people, so thank you all very much. I'll be counting on you in the future too.

This volume goes on sale in July, and the story takes place from early summer to autumn, so I'm thrilled to see how the seasons have synced up. What a happy coincidence!

The serialized releases never match the actual season, so I drew the preceding two-page spread to match with the real world. Without any connection to the story, the sakura trees are in full bloom! I have to say, I like that illustration, but I was never satisfied with the color illustration of Makomo and the others for chapter 9, so I put them on the back cover of this volume.

I suspect volume 3 will take place from autumn to winter. Nothing is slated yet, though, so here's hoping it gets the green light!

STAFF

REGULARS
Nagashima
Kantaro Kumano
Keisuke Futta

HELPERS
Kojiro
Tachi Biwa

SPECIAL THANKS
Saikyo Jump editor: Toide-san
The *Demon Slayer: Kimetsu no Yaiba* original manga team
Graphic novel editor: Abe-san
Designers: Deguchi-san, Abe-san
Original creator: Koyoharu Gotouge
All the readers!

Natsuki Hokami
帆上夏希.

Good work! This is Gotouge! Volume 2 of *Kimetsu Academy* is on sale! Here's a big thanks to Hokami Sensei, the editors, assistants, and readers! The number of characters playing a role is ramping up, making these pages more boisterous than ever!

As the fun continues to take off, I hope you'll come along for the ride!!

FIRST-YEAR TEXTBOOK DESIGNS FOR KIMETSU ACADEMY HIGH SCHOOL

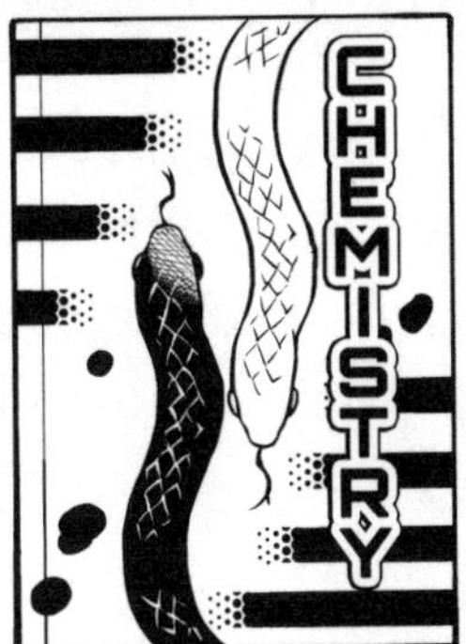

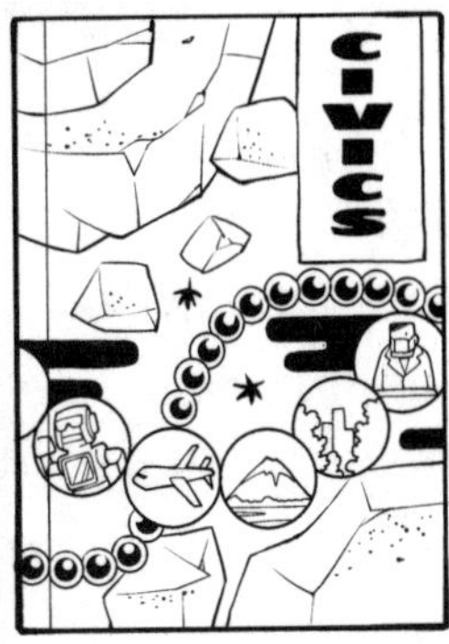

For a while, I only had a rough idea for these, but I asked my staff and they came up with proper designs. The other grades basically look the same.

You're reading the wrong way!

In keeping with the original Japanese comic format, *Demon Slayer: Kimetsu Academy* reads from right to left, meaning that action, sound effects, and word-balloon order are completely reversed from English order.

Check out the diagram shown here to get the hang of things, and then turn to the other side of the book to get started!